the shell of things

the shell of things

Poems by

Jacob Stratman

© 2024 Jacob Stratman. All rights reserved.
This material may not be reproduced in any form, published,
reprinted, recorded, performed, broadcast,
rewritten, or redistributed without
the explicit permission of Jacob Stratman.
All such actions are strictly prohibited by law.

Cover image by Eve Nam Oh
www.evenamart.com

ISBN: 978-1-63980-580-8

Kelsay Books
502 South 1040 East, A-119
American Fork, Utah 84003
Kelsaybooks.com

Contents

I.

First Hour	13
To Momento Mori	14
To the Japanese Wagtail	15
For the Amaryllis belladonna Who Dares to Bloom on this Mid-August Morning in Arkansas	16
To the Pileated Woodpecker	17
To Your Pain and My Declining Ability to See	19
To Your 13th Birthday	21
To the Blue Heron on Sager Creek in Early June	22
Ode to Attention	26
On Design	28
To Photic Sneeze Reflex	30
To Sincerity	31
To Cheonjiyeon Falls, 2018	32
To Chronic Tic Disorder	33
On Grace in Late August	35
A Prayer for My 15-Year-Old, Who Is Set Apart	36
To Loneliness	37
To Friendship	38
To Bread Bag Snow Boots	39
To My Inner Critic	42
Ode to the Tulip Tree on Your Birthday	44
Poem for My Sons When They Serve Lunch at Soup Kitchens	46

II.

the shell of things	49

III.

We Can't Draw What We Can't See	71
March Something, 2022: A Chorus	72
She Says I Should Write Something Scary	74
Tuesday, April 7, 2020	76
Liturgy	77
Resisting Metaphor	78
At 12	80
Tuesday, April 7, 2020	81
Where I Begin to Wonder About Awe and Fear	82
A Choreography of Loss, or What We Tell Ourselves	83
At the Student Art Gallery During Advent	84
Tuesday, April 7, 2020	85
She Called Me an Enneagram 3	86
Grandpa Worked at Glidden Paint for Over 30 Years	87
Tuesday, April 7, 2020	89
A Father's Aubade	90
A Poem for My Sons on Their First Kiss	92
Fishing After Church	93
Tuesday, April 7, 2020	94
Psalm 44: A Sunday Aubade	95
Learning to Kneel	96
A Gift	97
Tuesday, April 7, 2020	98

I.

First Hour

For C.R.C.

When they told me you died
on some random road outside
some town in Illinois in a drunk
guy's car you didn't know that well,
all I could think of was Roethke,
that barrel bear of a man
who could only think of himself
after he heard the news that his student
died, thrown from a horse, feeling
himself, his self *with no rights
in this matter, neither father
nor lover.* Forgive me.
                          It is airless
this morning: sticky, close. Cicadas
dive bomb sidewalks, screech
and shake when we accidently kick
them as we head to our cars. Worms
are half melded to the drying asphalt,
still reaching to the other side; some
are curled into themselves, crusted
brown like fried onions on top of church
potluck casseroles.
                       There's nothing
to marvel this morning, this late
in August, nothing winged or speckled,
nothing changing from one thing to another,
nothing to be born here but this guilt.
An opossum runs ahead under a streetlight,
one of her children falling off her back
and running back under the hydrangea.
I can't see how they will meet again.
I can't see how they will ever meet again.

To Momento Mori

When my son looks at Wyeth's "Airborne,"
he too quickly assumes the bird's dead.
Feathers can't just appear innocuous
in the air, floating there without some flesh
mangled, feathers matted, untangled
on the road—the notion that beauty
can exist without pain. Have we seen
too many chicken trucks barreling down
59 between processing plants in Decatur
and Noel for him to notice the shoreline,
whitecaps ushering wind, the cat-tailed edge
of the pond, so near the gray house,
it keeps a little to itself; all this green
in gentle undulation? He only sees
feathers, white and gray and black
and spread out, sporadic, fleeing,
moving away, never toward a thing.

To the Japanese Wagtail

after reading Hopkins in Pohang, South Korea

When my heart begins to stir in this place,
I don't think it will awake for daylight's
dauphin, even if I caught one on my morning
walk through dense woods, even if I looked
up to the soaring. Maybe too grand,
too high. But this bird. This black and white
dart wags its tail when it walks. This bird
flies like hills all around it—rolling
rice paddies, sandy conifers spilling
into the East Sea. This bird remembers
its home as a small fishing village,
not this steel city, not these scalped hilltops.
Its wings beat fast to gain what it loses,
then drop, only to beat again, to remain.

For the Amaryllis belladonna Who Dares to Bloom on this Mid-August Morning in Arkansas

When all you know of the stars is Orion,
the entire sky looks like war.
Even the moon, high up on this blue-black morning
wanes, retreats onto itself.

The entire sky looks like war—
swords and belts and shifting rectangles shaped like violence.
The moon wanes, retreats onto itself,
reflecting only a little light on the creek.

Everything is a sword and belt shaped for violence
when you're always playing the hunter.
Only a little light reflects on the creek,
and the tired cicadas screech for nothing.

When you're always playing the hunter,
you know where to find the fish in summer drop,
and you hear tired cicadas screech for nothing
but the inevitability of their future silences.

The fish will hide under rocks during summer drop
when all you know of the sky is Orion,
all you hear is the inevitability of future silences,
and all you see is the moon waning, retreating onto itself.

To the Pileated Woodpecker

Just outside of Moab, after a long night
of navel gazing, I looked up and out
to the tops of the cliffs, red rocks,
where the rising sunlight caught a hard line

and slowly, irreversibly lowered. I walked,
frozen and hungover, down the clay road
not knowing how long I'd have to keep
moving to meet the light, now changing

the rock face's color, sharing itself.
But I knew I couldn't remain still
in that tent, ill-prepared for early spring
frost, ill-prepared for the desert, ill-prepared

for ill preparation. I didn't know
much about hope then, but I knew I hated
being cold. I'm not there now, though,
but I'm cold, running down this road,

on the homestretch, before I wake up
the boys for school, thinking about Moab,
looking up at these fall pin oaks, the sunrise
cutting a hard line across their tops.

Above me, far away, the pileated
woodpecker looks like a buzzard—
red dot, dark body, patient in its rhythm.
The closest I'd come to this biggest

woodpecker was childhood Saturday
mornings jammied in front of the TV.
Now in this new place at this new age
on the woods' edge, I love its massive head

leading the rest of it from tree top to welcomed
tree top, immersed in sunlight, in all this hope,
yet it's sad to know I couldn't see it
clearly, that I misplaced it for something else.

To Your Pain and My Declining Ability to See

Wayne Thiebaud. Supine Woman.
1963, Oil On Canvas 36 x 72 in.

She presented you with her hair scrunchie
a week ago to wear on your wrist

in public, at school, when you're with the guys
at the pool, or lingering in the parking lot

just before soccer practice. It changed
your gait, this bluish-gray, silky iridescence,

billowy on your slim wrist—an awkward
corsage, a color full of morning fog

and promise. My students
tell me this is a thing now.

Like a ring, they keep saying. But today
you're sprawled on your bed,

diagonal, away from us. I think of Thiebaud's
"Supine Woman." She's flat on her back

on white, lots of white. Tired of being her.
Close up, the lines are thick, so straight-ish,

she can't move a tick—maybe she doesn't want
to move—her eyes held straight up—the lines

thinner around her thighs, her shape, her white dress,
barely visible, separate from all the space,

all the tenable white. But we know
that these lines, any lines, tell us nothing

but that they are there. Yes, you're her opposite,
in form, too, your head stuffed down deep

into the bed, on top of the blanket your mom laid
there to warm you this past fall—the same

scrunchie color now not on your wrist,
not anywhere I can see. When you turn

over, tears rest, stilled
in the corner of your eyes, thick

and obvious—like his paint, like those lines—
but only to the one who chooses to stand

close enough to begin to see, especially
to the one who chooses to attend

to the lines, on this bed,
usually so thin.

To Your 13th Birthday

The ball you kick in the backyard touches
Everything. Yet, no one discovers truth;
It is revealed. The house will shake, your mom
Will yell from inside. Fence boards broken show
Their allegiance to your developing,
Sharpening passing skills, your strength; the goal's
Net in paled tatters can't hold anything
You send it anymore. The ball you kick
Touches everything: the now shattered bird
Feeder; power lines; your brother's turned head;
All of the neighbors' backyards and a few
Of their dogs; each tree and many flower
Beds; the herb garden; the aluminum
Awning, dented, now housing a mother
Red-robin, neither amused nor annoyed
By the ball you tend to kick everywhere.
No one discovers truth; it is revealed.
Though nothing's revealed without kicking first?
What but your mom's love can ever allow
The backyard's slow, methodic destruction?
She knows this is the only way you know
To operate. You will touch everything.

To the Blue Heron on Sager Creek in Early June

This afternoon's newly issued
tornado watch doesn't touch

everything, just everything
in our viewing area: the little

league baseball game already
in the fourth inning; the church

garden party downtown;
the RV park just north of the Illinois River;

all of the cars and chicken trucks
on 59; the orange and blue speckled

panfish congregating under the uprooted
oak that floated down the creek

to our favorite hole after the last storm;
the donut shop on 412 we visit

each Friday morning; the dogwoods
and redbuds losing their celebrity

to the spring green in the woods;
the casino nearby, always in the news

when storm chasers drive in, park,
and watch the sky tinge green,

a murkier, more poisonous hue
than the trees it now threatens,

the trees it may uproot and throw
into houses, toss knowingly

among cows in the fields,
slide down creeks on top

of brown waves, or simply lay
across streets like a parent putting

a child to bed after a long night
crouching down in the hallway

closet. The radar on the screen
bathes all that I can see out the window

in a fading yellow, never promising
it won't turn red. Yet, the oriole—

flaming orange bird hopping branches
on the hackberry tree out back

ignores the feeder below, my soft
steps closer to it, even the danger

possibly approaching from the west,
southwest. We've never met,

but I've imagined this bird often—
an old man sharing an orange

with a neighbor on a day close
to the skin like this one, wiping

his brow with his sleeve, swapping
lies, and paying little attention

to any weather promised or predicted.
It's a dream realized, standing in front

of this oriole. And, this morning
you told me you're scared for Isaiah.

People will be mean to him when he's older
because of his dark skin, you prophesied

as we rounded a little bend in the creek,
standing shin-deep in the coolness

of our time together, just before we saw
the blue heron stand at attention

on the shore with the sky already announcing
its nefarious plans for the day, water

beginning its summer drop, bass finding
it harder to hide, fat crawdads

zipping backwards between the rocks,
tadpoles sprouting legs and shrinking tails.

Yet I carried my pole anyway
and you had your net, but they both stayed

on our shoulders, and our feet stayed flat
on the green slick slate beneath us

as we attended to the heron behold
and be held by everything around it.

We didn't want it to move yet,
as if the whole world would crack

and separate when the bird decided to leave
the log on this slight bend in the creek,

on this day that promised destruction,
in this life that isn't safe

for those we love, where tornado watches
touch everything we can see.

Ode to Attention

One of the windows in the living room frames a chestnut tree, now changing over to yellow. It's late October, and green is fading, not the same sharpness, newly minted green as March. And it's tired, having been on display for so many months, just losing its will to hang on, but hang on to the leaves it does, and it will for another month or so. Waiting are the growing splotches of yellow, red, orange. Nothing dramatic here in the Ozarks, just a nod of what it could be, perhaps. Today, I'm attempting to attend to this chestnut's mature green through this window—green that's seen a few things. The afternoon, predestined, western breeze knocks more of its bounty to the ground, scattered right on the woods' edge. Containers of chestnuts on the kitchen counter are set to roast, but it's the limbs and blue sky breaking through, and the timed mixture of fledgling yellow and feigning green that draw my attention so close to another election in the middle of a pandemic on the last day of our son's quarantine from school. It's just enough, these seven square feet of hope—fixed right now in expectant change, in anticipation, green moving to yellow without pain or reluctance. But how can you attend to what's present when your back hurts with weight of the past? The raccoon is what I remember. We'll lose an hour soon, and the blue moon's already begun its retreat inward, enough spectacle for one month. Ragged, like the boys' fall coats stuffed in the way-back of the dark closet for months, it crawled out of the trash bin, the slow sun already beginning its obedience. Maybe it didn't notice calm dawn race against the sky, lighting up the tops of the oaks and maples. Stretching all four spindly legs, without any urgency—thin, real thin—not in any hurry to get to bed or to find its family back in the woods, certainly not in a hurry to run from me or even turn back in attack. Like loneliness. It worries me, to think on it now, in front of this window filled with colors, to remember its heart just not in it much—no real desire to be a raccoon. It was a mild, clear morning, and there were mounds of the week's trash.

The kids even tossed in some pizza scraps the night before. It seemed like a pretty good day to be a raccoon, all things considered, but it didn't even look like it thought about its life much at all. I've been avoiding mirrors lately, too, I guess—any kind of sharp reflection. Here, I project on this raccoon instead of attending to this chestnut tree, framed and present, fading slowly from green to yellow. It's embarrassing to say how old I was when I learned leaves are most beautiful right as they die.

On Design

The Lego box is filled
with bodies: heads, hair,
hands, torsos, legs, capes,
assorted armor. It creeps
me out a bit, looking
into this box, when you
retrieve it, laying your body
flat, reaching, fingertips
straining to grab it, pulling
it toward you like a god
back from break.

So many fragments:
the disembodied,
the dismembered, the dissed.
It's an unmarked grave—
playtime's war ditch
way back there under the bed.
But you love these Lego.

You sit down at the box
and begin the work
of repair for the new day's
narrative. Harry Potter's body
will need Spiderman's face;
a police officer's vest with a lizard
king's legs, holding Chinese
throwing stars will begin
to see the world
through Michelangelo's eyes.

Velma's hair on Voldemort's
head with Batman's cape
on Wildstyle's jacket-body
will hold a hammer,
will hold a position
in your universe that fits
and mends, realigning
the brokenness in the box
in ways I can't understand,
but is needed to carry out
your plans for all of them
to prosper.

To Photic Sneeze Reflex

Each time we are called out of the car to face the sun, after having spent time in the shade, we respond with a sound offering—six or seven sneezes, our chorus of cacophony on a bright day. It is, I've been told, a genetic confusion of signals—these misfires making an announcement all their own. These sneezes are mistakes, I've read. There are no impurities in the nose to release and reject. The brain gets it all wrong. Maybe a change in light intensity or over-sympathetic body parts? Perhaps a product of the Fall—the trigeminal nerve a hot mess—too crowded, too many signals to manage. When you see us, though, a man and his two sons get out of a car, leave a building, or walk outside to check the mail, we'll begin sneezing at the sun, and you'll wish you were made of such mistakes—made of such tangled synapses, these automatic responses to light with bowed heads of obedience, sounds of our unplanned, unprepared praise, thanks, adoration.

To Sincerity

A cento for Abed Nadir

I much prefer being entombed alive
in a mausoleum of feelings
I can neither understand nor reciprocate.
We're at the mercy of each other
and ourselves. I can tell life from TV.
TV makes sense, it has structure, logic,
rules, and likeable leading men. In life,
we have this. We have you. That's why
there has to be forgiveness on both sides.
When you really know who you are
and what you like about yourself, changing
for other people isn't such a big deal.
I guess I just like liking things. Cool.
cool cool cool. I see your value now.

To Cheonjiyeon Falls, 2018

It's raining. I'm holding a pink umbrella,
you're holding it together ten months in,

our youngest, just before we pay fifteen
bucks at the ER to check the golf-ball

sized lump on his head after dancing
on a wet picnic table, holds himself

up, the same height as the grinning grandpa
stone next to him—basalt totem, welcome

symbols—sprinkled all over this volcanic
island, promising young couples baby

boys if they rub their flat, shined heads.
The four of us, stilled, look photoshopped—

dropped on top of beauty not ours to claim—
standing off-center, in front of a slick

bridge, as spring green cliffs take over.
A holy dragon lives here, we're told, deep

in the basin of the waterfall. Past
villagers wept for rain. All prayers answered.

The waterfall is not in this photo,
but we have others, several mirrors held

close to remind us of the ~~seared~~ sacred,
the heavy monsoon rain in April

where we learned to receive
answers, where we learned to pray.

To Chronic Tic Disorder

This morning, I watched a robin hit a window
and land quickly on the concrete below,

twitching without much movement
—its nervous system wrecked, spent,

and I remembered you, my chronic tic,
my restless shoulders, head, and neck.

When life was still, you couldn't be.
The doctor called you nervous energy—

something to run away, work out in gyms.
You arrived when stress was high or in

the waning of late afternoons
while I attempted rest with a book.

Later I learned to hide you from stares
with neck rolls and longer hair.

With unnecessary stretches, I passed,
mostly, for a body in control, unless

someone caught me relaxing,
reading in the library, watching

TV, or daydreaming. As a kid,
mom thought all I needed

was a haircut. She didn't realize
you were around. Neither did I.

When I first called you by name
in the locker room after a soccer game,

Buz didn't hear well, asked quickly
what that shaking had to do with a dick.

Still, we've been together many years,
and now you're not as willing, as eager

and excited to be in the spotlight,
to attract attention, to be in sight.

I've stopped taking meds
made to hide you, made to make

me normal; it is good not to fight
you anymore, not to seek even light

control over you. I am not in the mood,
the business, really, to make you good,

make you disappear. The bottle sits on a shelf—
a declaration not to try as hard to erase myself.

On Grace in Late August

She uses the dishwasher
only to dry what she washes
in the sink. She looks out across
the dry-brown backyard grass,
probably crinkly under foot,
like walking on potato chips
in the carpeted den, just to notice
her son's square garden, framed
by railroad tie fragments
housing rot and yellow jackets,
with its single jalapeno
or spotted Beefsteak hanging
heavily, waiting for him
to free them from the heat,
from the deer. No one's around
her now, anywhere near the kitchen—
the sun high, a spotlight, inviting
her gaze on the garden. It will be
years before he confesses
his sins at the counter,
to be absolved, just in front
of this sink where she promises
to wash peppers and tomatoes
that tend to die on the vine
on this heat-drenched square patch
of garden in the back, still
in view, stilled as she hums
hymns and waits for dishes to dry.

A Prayer for My 15-Year-Old, Who Is Set Apart

He won't come out of his room very often—
only to eat what we've prepared, only to receive
love that doesn't always look like anything he wants,
yet time is a friend of the God who creates it.

He won't come out of his room very often,
or speak in complete sentences or listen
long enough to attend to the beauty of silences
yielded here, prepared just for him. Not yet.

He won't come out of his room very often,
out of himself very often, but we will wait,
leaving this space empty of our wishes
You will fill with hope, with Your self.

To Loneliness

The flag at half-mast flails like an abandoned
nest, points now due east, due to me, perched
here in evening dusk at the end of the bench
in this dugout, absorbing a scalloped sky
of gray, growing black and pink, mixed
underneath like wet bottom feathers
on a barred owl after eating crawdads.

The setting sun loses its battle
to the storm. A row of aluminum bats
lean against the chain-link fence,
waiting their turn. Called to the plate, I grab
the fat bat, only wooden one,
the one I need, at night, in this storm—
my grace—even if heavy to swing true.

To Friendship

A cento for Stevie Budd

Sometimes I forget what life was like
before I knew you. I'm incapable
of faking sincerity. You're only
this happy when you have gossip
or there's something in the news
about Oprah. They do give me a small
weekly stipend for hanging out with you.
What you lack in most things, you make up
for in unsubstantiated confidence.
Because you're having boyfriend issues
and this is my reluctant attempt to try
and be supportive. I know everything
about you, about your history, your family,
and I'm still here. Look at this place.
                                            You've won.

To Bread Bag Snow Boots

The kids with money
wore brand new Moon Boots
on a Tennessee
fifty-year snowstorm
in January
tramping our iced streets
in all their shiny,
bold iridescence:
blues, greens, and silver.
Mom would set me up
on the Formica
kitchen countertop
and tell me to put
on my white, tube socks.
She covered me
with more socks, several
pairs, the tops red-striped,
maybe blue, reaching
just above my knees,
the sock heels,
small cotton bubbles,
puffing up a bit
over my dry calves.
She grabbed old bread bags
from the drawer and slipped
them over layers
of sock, wrapped masking
tape around the tops—
the brown stripe, now this
homemade boot's only
color.

Out the door
she'd send me and my
brother, equally
suited, equally
prepared for the snow
and cold that comes once
a childhood here
in this hot city,
only not before
she put more striped socks
on our stick hands,
up to our elbows.
I can't see much
else in memory's
picture—what else we
wore. Did we have coats
or hats or just layered
long-sleeve, cotton shirts
or mono-chromed sweats
we got from older
boys in our youth group?
When we got them, later,
Moon Boots, much after
their moment—these gifts
from the generous,
waiting for us there
on the front porch door
with other old clothes
for us to pretend
newness—with the sheen
a little dulled, cracked,

Mom would help us stuff
our heels down in black
holes, hurry us out
with the whispered truth:
poor kids; best stories.

To My Inner Critic

You are not mean, overly harsh, or rude,
Especially in public places. Thanks
For keeping quiet. You're reasonable.
You let me know what I can't do, who I
Can't be or become, and you're always here—

Every step of the way. You protect me.
You save me from rejection. You keep me
Safe from harm and humiliation. You
Remind me that I am not ready yet,
That I will never fully be ready.

You may, at times, overstate your case,
Turning each proclamation more anxious.
You do, please forgive me, on occasion,
Become slightly irrational. But, yet,
You stay strong and persist. You have my best

Interest in mind, I know, and, here and there,
You sound a little like people I love.
I know that we will continue to be
Together for many more decades. Yet.
Please listen. You will tell me, as you read

This draft—I can hear it already—not
To submit this poem, not to make
It public. You will tell me to look hard
At my Excel spreadsheet, the one you helped
Me create, with all of the rejections.

You will tell me this isn't a poem,
Just an echo chamber, flat sentiment,
A poetic selfie. You tell me
No one will damn well believe me anyway,
Me being male, white, employed. You will ask

Me to recognize my limitations,
My finitude. You will say these things
In various registers, pitches, and idioms;
Yet, to believe you, I need to see
All of it. I need to see your love.

Ode to the Tulip Tree on Your Birthday

I put bricks around it
so I wouldn't mow it down.

We were told it would grow
fast, but now that it reaches

far past the roof, I realize
I'm not quite ready to look

up so soon at its height—
to wonder if it could outgrow

the space it's placed,
and I fear it's not far

enough away from the wood
fence, the neighbor's bully

mulberry, the overhead wires.
I know the grand flowers

we'll admire won't come
for several years,

but the broad leaves,
little saddles, appear

broader, more themselves.
I clip a few low-hanging

branches so it won't look like
some untended, roadside bush.

It's quite possible it will stand
high above the houses

and become the largest
tree on the block, dwarfing

pin oaks, shortleaf pines,
but is that why it's there—

to tower, to outshine,
to compare? We might

convince ourselves we want
a little more shade in that part

of this small yard—a protector.
We might agree it's a bit too trite

to want an object that reminds.
We might believe it's far too simple

to know, to hope you've planted,
watered, tended a symbol.

Poem for My Sons When They Serve Lunch at Soup Kitchens

When my Uncle Ron walked into the church
kitchen ten minutes before the annual
youth group luncheon, wearing that shirt

*Eat your rice burner Put your ass
on some class Ride a Harley,* the two
old ladies, wrist thick in cream

of mushroom soup, green beans,
and fried onions, thought he was one
of *the homeless.* They scampered:

one after the pastor, my father,
his kid brother; and the other
after a ham sandwich and a Tab.

He would always just show up
"on his way to sell ketchup popsicles
to women in white," Pop would say,

"looking like Grizzly Adams."
This time, with his bike parked outside
the front door, the one painted red,

he ate the sandwich and sipped
the Tab at the head table
of the annual youth group luncheon

at Second Presbyterian Church, wearing
that shirt and that shit-eating grin
your grandma called the S.E.G. in polite company.

II.

the shell of things

"What can an outsider know except / the shell of things?"
—Maxine Kumin, "On Visiting Flannery O'Connor's Grave"

*

On the seventh day, although small,
he did something for another, enough
of something to receive a thank you.

Six days of receiving, of collecting,
he's now able to say it's nothing,
but he knows that it's everything

to contribute to the wholeness
of another. He's created nothing
for six days, he's brought nothing

out of nothing. He's only lain fallow—
a body continually at rest, he thinks
now, and only now, that he's accepted

gratitude. He's making something
on the seventh day—just getting started
like a rice field that can offer

the golden harvest to the farmer,
a shallow lake filled with rain water
that makes more room for the fish,

or his son, who, with his back straight,
looks directly at the stranger, translates,
intercedes for the father: it's enough.

*

He teaches here just below the prayer room,
hidden plainly on the roof where hymns
and chants and mystic paralanguage

mix with classroom lectures clanging
over hyper-amped microphones. In front
of the window, he sees the Pacific,

the East Sea, a sliver of blue or gray,
less than an inch, when he winks and places
his thumb and forefinger in front of his face,

as if holding a peanut before cracking
it or trying to measure the distance
of his discomfort, his awkwardness,

or like a god holding it all together,
or attempting to, as he breathes slowly
to contain his selves, but he knows that just

his forefinger covers the speck of ocean
between the two buildings and above
the dense woods beyond the window

where he stands three stories above the magpies
chattering and cackling at each other.
Job's Tears, just poured, too, reminds him

that he's not home—reminds his students
that he's old. He knows that the silent
sliver is not imagination—it's the sea,

that winking or covering it up
with his finger doesn't affect the millions
of miles of water teeming with things

he's just begun to think of as food.
But he can, if he wishes, put a finger
on its entirety when it grows too big.

                *

He searches for a word—the color
of the rice fields here in October,
Chuseok day. Golden seems most accessible,

easily connected to the wheat fields
he's seen in Kansas, but not the color
of the gold-finch in March, newly arrived

from winter. Not the sandy blond hair
of his son waving in front of him
on this narrow road between fields.

Crayola might suggest orange, yellow,
maize, dandelion, or maybe golden-
rod or sunglow when the day is bright

like this one, but the rice field resists
the only language he can offer.
Yellow perhaps is the color a child

or a foreigner might choose. He throws
his hands out in front of him over these fields
and pleads for a color, a chosen word

for a finished season, for the only
harvest of the year on this tiered hillside
near the sea under the blue sky—the same

blue that answers prayers, responds to chants
and petitions, that lunges, that rests,
that hugs every living thing at its end.

       *

He can't feel his mouth most days
after the third bite. He likes to watch others
eat, but just before the next, he blows

on his *kimchi jjigae* like he would
a roast right out of a Sunday crockpot
or a spoonful of chicken soup on cold,

blue days. He's told to put rice in the hotpot
to calm the spice; he's told to avoid anything
red, anything that doesn't taste like home.

       *

He thought rice cakes were bigger and flatter,
stale starch mixed with assorted paper
products, not these little balls—pink and green

and yellow, still warm, filled with red bean paste,
chestnuts, or sesame, tasting like deep
childhood memories he longs for, like stories

with clever rabbits, noisy magpies,
priestly dragons, and greedy lions
he wishes to be told, to understand.

       *

Walking around the market, he can't read
the air well. He asks too many questions,
he requests too many words, he always thinks

that one word is equal in weight to other
words—that language anchors everything.
He wants too much eye to eye contact.

To see is to love, he defends. To look
in the face is to recognize, to welcome,
he pleas. He can't read the air well enough

here. He smiles too much, his nods and bows
are too shallow, too deep, and his heart sleeps
each mid-day. He can only see the shell of things.

       *

He's wrong. He's been wrong all day.
He can't even apologize without being
wrong, saying I'm sorry to the wrong

person in the wrong manner, and now
he's wrong for using the wrong word
for bean paste, as he looks at rows and rows

of rice cakes in the window of the little
shop around the corner from where he buys
the wrong kind of vinegar and soy sauce

and the wrong kind of seaweed,
after he's just told a new friend how fun
it will be to make *kimbap* because it looks

so easy, and her tightened jaw told him
he's wrong—the same face this store owner
now makes as he asks if the filling

in the beautifully made yellow and green
rice cake balls is *doenjang.* Instead,
should he have used *patso* or maybe

chapssaltteok, or should he have just said
danpatso, he thinks later looking
at the list of words on the webpage

of terms and phrases that helps him be
more wrong each day. His language is wrong,
so he just guesses, grabs a package, bites

into the first ball in the very same
hopeful hesitance that he approaches
heart-filled chocolates each February

back home, and he chooses wrong.
But he knows, has always known,
what sesame tastes like on buns or crackers

or just the seeds in baseball dugouts; yet,
it's never felt like this—a squirt, a shot
to his tired palette, usually so wrong.

*

He rests here under the tall pines, under
fat pigeons on a low branch far away
from gray and greying buildings, unfinished

concrete train tracks reaching north, here with quiet
words next to a burial mound, next to columns
of rounded stones, pillars of prayer along

the path deep in the woods, next to the sea
surrounded by waxing sounds
of worship and his waning impulses.

*

Unlike Hansel and Gretel or Shadrach
and friends, he willingly crawls
into the furnace, the black-boxed

tunnel that leads into a large stone
cylinder kiln, not sure if he is preparing
himself for sacrifice or initiation

or both at 176 dry degrees. He sits
in sweat on hemp mats surrounded
by *ajummas* and *ajossis,* the aunties

and uncles frozen in prayer, maybe,
or in memory, keeping the heat
from finding new places on the body

to rest, breathing calmly but intentionally,
breathing the heat, breathing the darkness,
breathing shared air still enough to see

the common particles of human
debris, breathing in each other.
He has his face stuffed inside his shirt

breathing in the remaining air he brought
with him, most of him still outside, still
wondering, still unsure if it's good

to crawl into an oven—if it's good
to follow the others inside a place
where most of you is left behind.

*

He joked when he arrived he was glad
to leave tornadoes behind for a while.
He was ready to enjoy a fall

and spring without paying attention
to the mixing cold and warm fronts, to the shapes
of storm clouds in the west southwest,

to stillness and silences of birds,
to the sky's sinister Crayola yellows
and oranges. He was glad not to sleep

in his closet. When the earthquake hits,
and the tremors continues for weeks,
and the talk of potential causes

of underground missile testing
and geothermal drilling continues
for weeks after that, and he jumps

and twitches at every slammed car door
or passing truck, he finds himself longing
for home—the opportunity to wait

in the known potential of tragedy,
in the busyness of preparation,
in the perceived safety of knowledge.

He longs to hear the words Doppler,
echo hook, wall cloud—to hear sirens
wail, calling him back to the northeast

corner of the house away from windows
and outer walls. He longs for a trauma
he can understand.

*

After the earthquake, after the shocks
of being displaced and playing refugee
for a couple of days on church floors

and in tourist hotels, he returns, clutching
nothing tightly anymore, to the newly
cracked and cracking apartment. His boys

relearn the paths, walking around piles
of bricks, away from bulging walls, above,
up the stairs, and into their rooms to make

guns out of Duplo bricks, to build rifles,
several pistols, even a sword or two,
a cache of grenades, and they run around

the place dying and yelling and being
reborn and dying again, bricks willy-nilly
across the living room, bricks under the couch,

in the kitchen, and on all the beds,
while their mom, still gripping metaphors,
says despair, despite what theologians
may say, *is a mildewed tent,* while she keeps

track of the tremors on her calendar, noting
their seismic weight, the time of day, the spaces
in between. She counts days between the earth's

contractions. Each whisper of a tremor
doesn't mean necessarily they will cease,
that each rupture is a release of tension,

she has read and repeats, reads and repeats.
She is like one ready and frightened
to be a mother, looking for patterns,

constructing ways out of fear,
out of ignorance, out of anxiety,
away from the *dumb show.* She's building

something she hopes to understand. The bedroom
door doesn't shut now, not completely,
not as it should, and the front door won't lock.

It's misaligned, and she sweeps more dust
and plaster chips every day. Nothing's working
as it should. He reminds them this shaking

should not surprise, but the boys are ready
for complete fallout, while she waits, calculates,
and records. Waits, calculates, and records.

*

In the middle of prayer, people still
and shaken from the earthquake, a chair
collapses—the one thing that still holds

their belief, their attention—holds it so
that he hasn't given chairs much thought
until he sees one collapse. Who approaches

a chair quietly, hesitantly,
reverently? Who wonders if chairs
will neglect, reject, stop supporting,

stop existing as themselves?
No one among us resists belief
in a chair, he whispers to no one,

as prayer hums, crashing sounds linger.
A metal chair loses its integrity,
and he's losing his faith in any thing.

*

He's not a believer in much these days,
not even moved by the monk's chants
in the lower temple here in this crowded,

rewashed complex; yet, he wants someone
to lead him higher, past the middle
temple with its loads of gifts up the steep

stone stairs to the high temple where no monk
is seen today, just thousands of glowing
Buddhas in tight rows without shadow.

*

He begins to hum into the silence,
several bars of his favorite Christmas
hymn. Hum might be too melodic

to describe soft sounds that begin
in reaction, in response, in impulse
while doing the dishes and sweeping

or attempting to sweep sticky rice
from under the table. It's March:
the sun is setting later; he's still

tired, half-spent. The fat, wet snow
this morning, white and full of reflecting
dawn, has now puddled and slushed itself

out of existence. He hums regardless
and winces a bit that he doesn't know
the word for rose in any other language

but his own. He's forgetting how to see
it in full bloom; he's learning to hide
behind bows, scripted phrases of politeness.

    *

The magpies hop as one across the street,
chattering and cackling at each other—
the white-tipped wings you only see

in flight, white shoulders, white breast,
metallic shine of wings and tail feathers,
most intelligent bird, quite possibly

capable of grief. It's good to be
over here where they bring good fortune,
where they outwit lions and tigers,

where they dine on rice cakes and sesame
seeds. The pigeons stay in trees, mostly,
but magpies spend their time on the streets.

It's clear he needs somebody near,
and the stories tell him they will cry
with you—they will you bring good news.

    *

He notices trumpet vines sculpted
like trees planted against blues,
reds, yellows of collapsing brick walls

decorating homes in fishing villages.
Back home, they crowd wire fences.
In ditches, they're cut down by mowers.

*

The dogwood and redbud blooms in March
are what he misses—the speckled hope
among the resting bare branches, the whites

and reds among the bared brown hills, crags,
and valleys of his home, but he only notices,
considers, believes this longing now

on this walk around this lake in the woods
between hills staring at the fainted
purples he doesn't know, cannot name,

winking at him, these trees, these azaleas,
he's later told, in the sunlight, cutting
through the pines and a few oaks resting bare,

the same as home as far as his eyes
will allow him to look up the hill,
but it's those cherry blossoms in their celebrity

a week or so away from crowding the stage
when he will join the masses walking
along the streets in parks to see

planted city trees, planned beauty,
picnics under the blooms, taking pictures,
posing, chasing flowers in the wind

with his sons, and then he'll forget
these purple dots, these woods blinking
in color like he forgets dogwoods

and redbuds against the cherry blossoms'
arrival, when strangeness overwhelms,
envelopes, and invites him again.

*

He knows he needs glasses, most images
becoming a little bit blurrier, harder
to identify and comprehend than before

he arrived. He didn't notice the old
woman, full smile and a gentle nod
on the city bus, handing his son

a pack of gum and a greasy black bag,
her lunch, they assumed, of fried chicken,
the whole bird split, flattened, fried. More fry

than flesh it looked when they got home
and gathered around the bird on plastic plates
in the center of the table, next to half glasses

of juice. They gave thanks for it, for her.
They ate and hoped to remember, to see,
to recognize, to understand, to love.

*

He looks for an estuary, stillness
between the river's roar and the ocean's
wide swallow. He knows where it is

on the map—the steel mill covers most
of the land here, the space that is both
and between. He desires to watch the water

birds moving inland from the vastness
of the Pacific, looking for the clams
and shrimp, nesting in the resting streams.

He knows from reading that this mixing
can be a volatile space, too much salt,
too much sediment. He will look

for life in abundance, the fragility
and fertility, but, he knows
he can't see deep enough to notice

how birds capture small fish
or where crabs hide. He only sees
what is there clearly in front of him.

*

When he finally finds his son who ran
away from him in a crowded aquarium,
they were taking turns posing with the boy

in front of a pair of manatees,
this group of smiling, middle-aged women,
their peace signs angled in toward their dimpled

faces, or open palms resting on blossoming
cheeks, or pairs of hands connected to form
a heart's shape, the leader's index finger

stroking the boy's hair—a group photo
with this blue-eyed, tow-headed, cow-licked kid
who thought they were there to see fish behind glass.

*

The fields are flooded, the rice planted.
He can only think of mosquitos, though,
that will come. The discomfort when he sits

for too long and collects red welts and bumps,
the limited time now to wander the woods'
paths and rice roads, the lake's shores,

not the green of the young shoots, firm
but flexible in this late spring day breeze,
not the white crane in the stilled water

in the corner of the field statued there
against the blue sky, against the dark pine
forest like pots he's seen in markets,

in museums, not the cuckoo birds' high
calling out of trees to each other,
like clocks telling time to begin—the cycle

again, not the rippling water performing
obedience to the wind, the rice
in unison with everything around

it soon to be hidden, covered
by flourishing stalks. He can't even see
what this scene will become later, the thickness

of the crop, the changing colors, the harvest.
He just knows what you get when water
pauses, stays still for too long—what it feels

like when air becomes hot and wet
and buzzing keeps you inside,
when stillness keeps you inside,

    *

He isn't dyslexic, but he tends to read
scared as sacred. He won't walk too close
to the mounds, burial sites tucked, hidden

toward the tops of forested hills,
but his little one is all too ready
to climb them, to pronounce his victory,

his authority, his self over these humps—
two breaching whales just now breaking the surface,
slanted on one side, the water of clipped

and cared-for grass sliding down their backs.
He knows the beautiful blur of sacred
and scared, the lean toward walking around

instead of through the love that denies
every path that may lead to lives
who aren't his to remember,

deaths that aren't his to mourn.
There's a blooming apricot tree
on a hill beside this path leading

to this burial mound. There are puddles
of pollen from the pine trees mixing
with rain, knocking down pillowy, pink

blossoms. His dreams don't have language,
just slow images of people walking
through woods of unmarked mounds,

looking for those they've left,
searching for those they can't find,
for themselves.

*

He tries to forget what he knew—
what he shouldn't have read before he left:
now I know only in part,

*then I will know fully even as I
have been fully known*. He can read
the alphabet now; he doesn't know

what he reads. He can speak one sentence;
he can't speak two. He can understand
how much to pay; he can't tell time. He can

identify a few birds in tall pines
where he walks in late afternoon;
he doesn't know their song, where their journeys

begin and end. He can greet his neighbors
each morning; he'll never know their hearts.
He can be polite; he can't love. He can't

more than he can. He doesn't know more
than he knows. And now that he returns,
how does he tell about a land he can't know

fully, when metaphors break quickly.
What muse does he invite to help him write
of the typhoon, the redstart, the *kimchi* pots?

Each utterance, each fragment must begin
and end, when he is wrong: *shillyeh hamnida.*
choesong hamnida. Excuse me. I'm sorry.

III.

We Can't Draw What We Can't See

For E.S. and ART 2413: Drawing 1

After receiving bad news, I watch
kids draw still life: plastic paled fruit, dusty
bottles, leather boxes, lanterns with faux
finish, copper kettles, everything draped
in gilded maroon. Masked students circled,
spacious music spacing against sickness.

One holds a view finder, leaning
on her drawing horse, trying to avoid
men—flaky busts of Homer or Aristotle.
She has her eye on a clock next to oddly
shined apples. Another, off by herself,
circle adjacent, mines a paper bag landscape—
ridges and rifts, creases, cracks, crinkles,
valleys, vaulted lines separating shade and light.

We can all hear the woodpecker: deadwood
deadwood deadwood. Late winter branches
stretch up against darkening blue, waning
daylight. A few, near windows,
look hard, point in competing directions.

A turkey vulture floats above. Someone calls
it an eagle. Too high to differentiate
baldness. No one here knows what kills
trees from the inside, but we all know
eagles are visible for another month
or so, and we forgive the mistake.
Too many buzzards circling all the time,
you often wish for difference.

In silent breaks, circled and spaced,
on a cold, late afternoon when light
is lowering, we attend to what we can't see
well—what we mistake for hope.

March Something, 2022: A Chorus

A hawk can't lift the dead
squirrel off the asphalt.
Driving home after errands,
I'm not quite close enough
to see under its wings, waving
empty-clawed. Scalloped?
Striped? Never mind.

Another tornado watch
today. It's difficult
to remember anything
we said to each other
that evening, our first date,
What we ordered? What
we wore? What we talked
about? Where we went
afterwards? Questions
we fear anyone asking.
What better way to judge
a marriage than by what
one (or two) can't remember.

Later, we can see it,
looking at the radar
separately on our phones:
a storm-line stretched
from Houston to Manitoba,
a bow bending north,
northeast. Spring peepers sing
in the marsh below, down the hill,
in the woods where the bobcat lives.

The underdog can't hold on,
so you turn off the TV—
one less sound to interpret—
leaving us just rain, frogs,
our collapsing memory,
forecasted danger, and thunder's
chorus—its bow to light,
surrounding all we can't hold,
and are only invited to witness.

She Says I Should Write Something Scary

Sun's only been up a couple of hours
and it's already 80, thick and getting close

even in the shade, with a torrent of cicadas
above me, all around, or maybe just a few

in harmony, sounding for a mate, perhaps
calling on this sizable storm, in the distance

here, just inside my periphery, climbing,
blotting the sun without any good sense

that weather of this magnitude should have
golden haystacks out front, near first vision,

like Heade would want, glowing a bit,
but there's no lightning or rain, yet,

just the heaviness of approaching darkness,
and I should be inside a museum gazing

at the sterility of such mass—the lack
of danger and urgency and fear—such potential

destruction next to simple haystacks,
but I'm here, under threat of a blackening

sky, stuck in a summer drop creek bed,
looking out for sunbathing copperheads,

and trying not to consider how frightening
it is to catch a fish, to reel it in and hold it

in my hands, especially the small ones,
with old spinner baits, that I may kill them—

that unconsciously, unconscionably, I won't feel
the hit, the subtle two or three tender taps,

that I won't set the hook fast enough,
and it will begin to take it in—all of it—

blood pooling on the inside of a small blue gill,
one of the three hooks buried into flesh

and I've forgotten the pliers, the tool I use
to help get me out of such dilemmas, my son

looking on knowing I'll fix it, knowing I'll find
a way to pry the hook out of the innocent,

no bigger than my hand, who hit the lure fast
and hard, darting out from beneath the slate rock

ledge, just below my feet, not a foot down,
before I could react right and set the hook

properly, but I'm failing, our blood mixing,
no metaphor, because I'm cutting myself

on the other two hooks, and too many minutes
are passing, too many tiny breaths are lost

before I'm able to rip it out with only a little
reminder of my blunder left on the lure.

I lower it back into the creek as I was taught
and let go—it sinking slowly beyond the visible,

even though my boy is convinced he sees
the fins move, convinced he sees it live.

Tuesday, April 7, 2020

Our son practices
for a disaster, his next
badge: tick bites
and burns, choking
victims, broken bones,
and hypothermia.
Not big enough to wrap
his arms around me
to find my sternum,
he stands on a chair
and beats my back
until I breathe
again, until I sing,
until I thank him
for saving me.

Liturgy

I've known two owls. One wore a bowtie
and Ben Franklin glasses, spoke affected,
academic English, and licked Tootsie Roll
Tootsie Pops until it all turned too much,
then took a bite. He could count, yes.
On Saturday mornings, we believed
he was smart but not patient.

The other performed smart in the group,
but he couldn't read, mixing *hipy papy*
for happy. He looked the part—erect,
professorial, perpetually right. Not smart,
but he played one on TV.

So, you can see I approach you early
this morning, after a run, with a little
apprehension and a lot of ignorance,
having heard your vowel extended,
echoed from high up in the darkness
of a hackberry at the parking lot's edge.

I don't know your name, your migration
patterns, mating habits, and you may think
it unfair of me to project comparisons
of train whistles and long wails of ship
horns on sounds you present before the sun
arrives, but here we are. You called.

I've responded, having learned
enough about you to know how
not to *talk to anyone who can spell
Tuesday.*

Resisting Metaphor

After reading Jen Grace Stewart, after listening to Mark Jarman, after running

Is it true: *poetry is a gesture inward,*
and prayer a gesture outward?
The poet seems sure in the interview
I listen to on an early morning
run, with sunrise beginning
to bounce life off haystacks, the color

of campfire marshmallows, color
like these fallow fields, welcoming me inward,
green coming to focus as day begins
to begin, and I'm stuck, neither in an outward
posture or accepting the invitation this morning
to reflect, intimate, or withstand an interview.

But what would the field ask if this were an interview?
How would the haystacks respond to the color
I choose to give them on this early morning
run? Must the metaphor always seep inward?
Does the sun care whether prayer is outwardly
gestured? O'Connor suggests ignorance is the beginning

of faith. I remember, once, standing creekside, beginning
to wonder, when I scared a bird just in view,
a black crowned night heron—the outward
expression of surprise and fear; the color
of attention; another invitation inward;
a symbol I ignored respectfully that morning.

It wasn't big, like hawks, the color of mourning,
I see on wires above county roads, beginning
their day in lament. Although I resist inward
movement of any kind these days, any interview
with myself, especially on these discolored
roads I run, I know I'm invited outward,

to see birds and haystacks, outwardly
themselves on any given morning,
but the memory of those heron's wings—working to color
everything for me, setting its self in flight, beginning
their motion before its body could begin an interview
with its own wings, even as I deflect (reflect?) inward—

urges prayer inward and outward—
asks me to interview the morning,
its beginning, my beginning, perhaps: a new color.

At 12

Among wicker chairs, waiting, facing
floor-to-ceiling windows high above

Lake Michigan, several hours before
sunset, he watches waitresses move

around the dining room, like sailboats
small at the horizon line, bathed in brown-

beige uniforms that fit in various
degrees of not fitting—college girls

whose boyfriends spend summers teaching
kids in the Amazon, who listen to Sun Records

at night in their poster-less bedrooms,
and give these girls Amethyst bracelets

on birthdays. He cups his crocheted
dragon under the table, open, close

to his belly, like receiving benediction—
the typical green, with red-fire wings,

and smoky nose—the one his great-aunt
made last summer sitting each evening

on the veranda, just beyond the tulips,
oranges and reds, already dulling

as the sun moves beyond their vision,
into the lake shine, while they both watch

gulls dive deep to retrieve stale bread balls
other boys on the beach toss after dinner.

Tuesday, April 7, 2020

It's a mostly cloudy evening,
the reflective glow
from the casino down the street
across the state line
yellows the sky like healing,
like memory. Like it, I think,
but not it. Not healing.
Not memory. But close to it—
the only thing I can link yellow
to on a night that seems boxed
in by lowering clouds, not white
and puffy, not inviting and grateful.
Simile is a prayer, petitioning
and pretending, an intimacy
that cannot exist here where the closest
we come to gold streets
is the yellowing clouds
from a casino's jumbo Tron
in a parking lot that sometimes hosts
storm trackers, tornado chasers.

Where I Begin to Wonder About Awe and Fear

I thought it was a nightmare. Indeed,
the image frightened me—a torso heaving,

its broad flesh covered in breathing eyes
from neck to waistline, face and arms blurred.

Canvassed in sweat or tears? There was a glistening—
a heat, a hard laboring, a proclamation.

When I awoke to the oblong moon,
winds blowing after the storm, already

poised to usher in the next, I stayed scared,
even as I tried to guess the being's

purpose: to haunt me, devour me, rest
upon my soul until I grew mad?

Now, though, when I remember
the eyes, all of those eyes on that body,

its pulsing presence, the memory
comes upon me with a different force:

like the eyes of a mother over her child's
crib, her posture's yearning, her shoulders

arrowed at protection—her eyes soft,
her breathing rhythmic, her grip tight.

A Choreography of Loss, or What We Tell Ourselves

after reading Ellen Pinsky

Each break-up: a reenactment of Freud's
grandson throwing the wooden spool on a string,
then retrieval—his only way to tend
with loss, to control it. Seems like the thing—
it's pretty easy to master, as long
as you have good hold of the rope: enough
will and guile to push and pull it along.
When you tire of happiness, the same stuff,
toss it well overboard. Stop seeing it,
pray it gone until you tire of sadness—
when it's quite a disaster—then bring it
back as you witness expanding gladness.
It's simple subtraction and addition.
Call it therapeutic repetition.

At the Student Art Gallery During Advent

For L.M.

A house   pink   on a beach

clouded   by ocean   sand   sky

satellite dish   like a hand

cupped   expecting   a blessing

Tuesday, April 7, 2020

The virus spreads
while we sit

in the back
watching

the spring green.
The preacher says

the church
has been socially

distancing itself
for decades,

maybe centuries,
so what's new.

Before the worm
is called to eat the vine

God brought forth
for Jonah, mad as hell

on the hill,
according to L'Engle,

the turtle chastises
the prophet:

*love is the most
terrible pain of all.*

*And you are afraid
of pain.*

She Called Me an Enneagram 3

Wherever's the opposite of laid back,
she says, is where you tend to play,
counting the weight of worth in stacks

of accolades and achievements; keeping track
of affirmations; constructing the day
in whatever's the opposite of laid back;

adjusting your approach, your attack
for each social event, each display
of counting the weight of worth in stacks

of admirers; setting goals that never lack
prestige, difficulty, or the briefest stay
against whatever's the opposite of laid back—

valuing being valued; hacking up the hacks;
loving only the lovely; making your own way;
counting the weight of your worth in stacks.

You don't work to be the best; instead, in fact,
You work to be the favorite and so remain
whatever's the opposite of laid back,
always counting the weight of worth in stacks.

Grandpa Worked at Glidden Paint for Over 30 Years

Martin Johnson Heade, "Newburyport Meadows," 1876–81

Say *bucolic* and see the neglected
child of bubonic and colicky.

It's not a pretty word. It's sickly.
It's its own throat-clearing. Is it COVID,

she wonders? No, it's just bucolic,
but still; yet, here it is in prose pairing

with this painting, saying what I can see
for myself: a massive scene of storm

and field and water and work. Heade's wetlands,
although partly shadowed are front and low,

marshy but mirroring the golden haystacks.
Is the storm stage left coming or going?

Despite the distant rain, light pronounces
work in the center of everything.

A valley of sorts—rock ledges and sloped
green keep us attending to the work

at hand. No sheep anywhere—the herdsmen
gone to another pasture, a previous

poem, maybe. The haystacks, like raindrops
or gumdrops, stand sentinel or symbolic

or just statuary. In the belly
of it all, the horse, almost small enough

to be mistaken for a smudge, waits
for the storm, or is glad to see it go.

Everything's so clean, sterile, washed
and renewed while the work keeps on.

The laborers too far away—just white
dots—to notice how their shirts can still be

so white after a day out in the fields
before or after a storm this size.

The soil seems inundated with Adam's
ale; I sure wouldn't call it dirty

water, not with all this bucolicky
beauty to absorb, to try to swallow.

Tuesday, April 7, 2020

The fire alarm chirps
falsely, like a coal mine
canary's first day
on the job—every silence
dangerous, toxic.
Our youngest sleeps,
despite the computer-voice—
fire fire—too immune
to computer voices,
too immune to threat.
Our oldest curses
the darkness, my foolishness.
You claw for my arm,
then sink into the night
when you feel my closeness.
We cry out like we're new
at this—the alarms and alarums—
like it's our first day
in the mine, like we don't know
the canary's already dead.

A Father's Aubade

I wish you mistook
the moon, for a hole,
a portal, feigning
but present in waxing
fullness against blue
sky, early morning—
a point you think
connects you to ancients,
mythologies you enjoyed
me reading late at bedtime.
But, you know
it's just the Earth's moon.
You understand a little
too much about its phases,
vast ocean tides,
the sun's influences.
Yet, I utter wishes
to you anyway in hope
mystery resides
still somewhere
under your floppy hair,
behind your black,
square glasses.
You roll your eyes
and go back
to perfecting
the left-footed Akka
in front of the goal
with tattered netting
you've been working
on for hours already.

I'm not all that good
at flinging myself
in the universe
of your interests,
but I know this orb
you sleep with at night,
worn out and dirty
after only a month's
use, is your soul's
portal I mistake
for a soccer ball.

A Poem for My Sons on Their First Kiss

A seasoned sixth grader spins the bottle

as if she brought it from home, had a name

for it, even its own place on some bookless

shelf. Ninevah looked pretty appetizing

as the wet, ordained mouth took Jonah prisoner

Fishing After Church

The poisonous ones, I've been told, will glide
completely on top of water. They hide

nothing, so always look closely
at their bodies, they say. If you just see

the slick head popping up out of the creek,
you're safe. Its jarring, though, when sleek

cottonmouths treat water like a sidewalk,
and you're trying to fish a little, talk

a little after a fall rain. What but Love
controls the elements? What but Love

treats water and its depth with such simple
disregard? You thought you knew these answers until

you watched a snake slip easily on top
of water—slide soundlessly, with no plop

or announcement, separate from laws
you knew to trust, whose cat eyes give you pause,

whose toxins keep your warm blood from clotting,
who keeps you confused and far from saving.

Tuesday, April 7, 2020

The birdfeeder's broken,
thanks to a wayward
soccer ball. Today just a few
days before the end of Lent.
It goes unnoticed. I pour
several pounds of black-oil
sunflower seeds and watch them,
this black joy, continue their path
downward through the hole
and on to the ash heap of shells.
The squirrels and pigeons
and juncos will gather soon,
once I go back in the house,
but that will be it for a while.
The feeder will sit and swing
empty for months, I'm sure,
before I buy another—the new tufts
will come covering the seeds.
I try to remember the broken
gumball machine in the mall
spewing treasure, hundreds,
with only one turn—rainbow sugar
bouncing in multitude on the tile,
calling kids from as far away
as Penney's, bathing them
in excess, maybe access,
but it never happened,
not that I know of.
Can you imagine
all that promise?
All that color?

Psalm 44: A Sunday Aubade

Spring begins to show itself through stained glass;
The burning bush's oranges and yellows
Behind the choir almost look inviting.
Some mother in the far back refuses
To leave, to remove her screaming baby

From the sanctuary this new morning
During the reading of Psalm 44.
The drowning liturgist reads on: *All day
Long my disgrace is before me, and shame
Has covered my face.* Disruption annoys

Us mostly. Resisting our shared glances,
We ignore the cries and wails and sup-sups.
We don't hear pain. We try not to listen.
*For we sink down to the dust; our bodies
Cling to the ground.* We straighten our straight backs,

Lift our chins, look forward at nothing here
In particular, refuse attention.
*Awake, Lord! Why do you sleep? Rouse yourself!
Do not reject us forever. Why do you
Hide your face and forget our misery*

And oppression? One might hear dry coughing;
One might feel restless movement in the pew.
Sure, one will certainly see the narrowed
Eyes of a few sopranos, but listen:
We try in earnest not to hear crying.

Learning to Kneel

The first time I stopped pledging allegiance
to the flag, my mom sang *Abide with Me*
and wept, the valley of death's long shadow
returned to my dreams, *on Earth as it is
in Heaven* grew heavy to hold, I fell
deep in love with the expanse of language.
Placing my right hand still over my heart,
swearing all my loyalty to a flag
didn't ring true, beautiful, as slipping
down the street to the creek, to the sweet spot
under the bridge, next to the wide weeping
willow's shade, where we'd all meet to skip rocks
or wade in bare feet looking for crawdads
and wonder around in God's solitude.

A Gift

After teaching Flannery O'Connor's "Revelation"

It's one of those box frames you get from folks
who don't know you very well—maybe two inches

deep, three and half inches tall, cheap wood,
no glass front, squared paper posing as its picture.

On this one, my name is underlined,
and an aphorism sits prophetically in the center:

*Make the one / who's been / left out /
your special / friend.* Then *Luke 6:31*

rests at the bottom: the one about not judging
people. When she gave it to me at the end

of our time together, I knew the words
were both affirmation and critique.

The old man I loved would call
it a mixed bag. Maybe she meant it

for harm—ridicule wrapped up as gift,
maybe a prize for trying, for good

hustle? So many years later, it remains
on a window ledge, surrounded by books,

just beyond this computer, still inside
my field of vision, still inside memory's

loop, and I can hear another woman in my mind
yell at God: "How am I a hog and me both?"

Tuesday, April 7, 2020

From where I sit in the backyard, I can see
the oak leaf hydrangea, now simply a stick
poking a foot out of the ground wearing
a single green leaf, a flag waving. You
are in the kitchen baking a cake

after making lime coconut banana muffins,
and the boys are not bugging us
or hurting each other. So I attend
to the fledgling, this shrub, not yet,
that needs very little from me.

We will wait for its dramatic white
blooms, its fullness, the green leaves
resembling the elder trees
around it. I know you're thinking
of people we can't see, the errands

we shouldn't run, the future we can't help
but nurture, but we were convinced the plant
died last summer, after you transplanted it
from your mother's garden two hours away,
and here it is, nothing much to look at,

but it's here after our winter of discontent,
our winter of waiting and wanting,
so we've been given this bare
and baring stick in the ground to notice,
to serve with our noticing.

Notes and Acknowledgements

In "First Hour," I quote from Theodore Roethke's "Elegy for Jane (My Student Thrown by a Horse)."

"the shell of things" is dedicated to my colleagues and students at Handong Global University in Pohang, South Korea, where I served as visiting professor from 2017–2018. Our time there was transformational, and I am forever grateful to the people who welcomed and shared their lives with us. The phrase *the shell of things* comes from a line in Maxine Kumin's "Visting Flannery O'Connor's Grave." The phrases *is a mildewed tent* and *dumb show* come from lines in Maxine Kumin's "Despair." At the end of the poem, I quote 1ˢᵗ Corinthians 13:12 from the *New International Version*. Lastly, I'm thankful to the many readers of this long poem who gave it their thoughtful attention as it journeyed through many revisions: Junmo Cho, Jern-lyn Chong, Ben Egerton, Brad Gambill, Patty Kirk, YounSook Na, and Melanie Pierce.

"To the Blue Heron on Sager Creek in Early June" received the 2021 Willie Morris Award for Southern Poetry—Poem of Distinction.

In "Liturgy," I quote from A.A. Milne' *Winnie-the-Pooh*.

I fell in love with Li-Young Lee's *Rose* the first time I read it. The structure of *the shell of things* is my gratitude to that book and Lee's work.

Much gratitude to the following journals where many of these poems first appeared: *kissing dynamite, FreezeRay, Ekstasis, Moria, 2 River, Autumn Sky Daily, Amethyst Review, Bearings Online, Spoon River Poetry Review, The Christian Century, Salt Hill Journal, Naugatuck River Review, softblow, Glassworks, Grey Sparrow Journal, Ekphrastic Review, Eunoia Review, Fathom, and Wordgathering*. Please read them and send them your work.

Several of these poems began as writing exercises in my poetry workshop at John Brown University. My thanks and appreciation to that writing space and to those students, especially the writing group that formed after the Fall 2021 semester: McKi, Kat, Mak, Santi, and Luke.

Special thanks to Holly for helping me with all things editorial to get this book ready for publication.

To Jules, Ben, and Jude for allowing me to write about particular parts of our lives, mostly expressed in ordinary time.

About the Author

Jacob Stratman's first collection of poems, *What I Have I Offer With Two Hands,* is a part of the Poiema Poetry Series (Cascade, 2019). He and his family live in Siloam Springs, Arkansas.

www.ingramcontent.com/pod-product-compliance
Lightning Source LLC
Chambersburg PA
CBHW030053170426
43197CB00010B/1500